Growth

Devon Gillespie

Nothing

I used to think this place I am in is nothing

I looked up the definition of it, it still came out to something

This place I was in was full of meaning and pup

I had to wait a while until these words had popped up

This nothing was still something, it was like a gift from distance

I think that wrapping these gifts is
something of great importance

You never know what will come but you can
think of it as the greatest thing since

Your interpretation of imagination is all in your head

This something is nothing, but only if you're dead

Your brain will release all of the thoughts that have been said

Then someone could take the messages that are read
and make it into something better instead

This nothing is nothing I see; when I live
to create, it's something to me

Media

Everybody is on their best behavior where there are cameras and vids

What would happen if you recorded war and showed it to the

kids?

I think if you did then those tiny soldiers will turn into tiny students

Those students will want to end it but they can't because it's just a game played by the masters

They turn into the old guys the reminisce of the same kid who wanted to change everything and fix all the disasters

Why did I want to cause so much conflict and turmoil?

Is it because of the things that I fought over, like food and oil?

I should try to understand why they're saving these things and then just go to bed

It was obviously for a good reason, because they did care

If there was a different problem, I am sure we could help them there

I didn't have to resort to pointless destruction

I didn't have to listen to misinformed instruction

I could have made my own choices

I could have not listened to the audience's voices

Cards

I know that in this game of love I never want to part

This deck of cards means nothing when I think of how to start

How do I play it now when I can see this change of heart?

It's surprising to say the least, this is something that I never foresaw

Should I be scared or excited? Or should I sit here in awe?

Should I smile at the amazing person you are?

Should I realize that even though you're away you're never really that far?

I've noticed now that just like me you will be a star

I know I shouldn't block your light; I just want to raise your bar

Magnificent is what you are to me, let's try and stack the cards

I can be the spade and you can always be my diamond

We'll mix our hearts and clubs together; we won't have to live in confinement

This is what I would call anxiety refinement

A pure and honest game in which neither of us are in fear

We could take a break and start over, just to make our heads clear

This game is all I want, I want to keep playing, this is a game I will always hold dear

Truth

Listen to that singing poet whenever they're around

Here are some good messages that if are looked at closely they can easily be found

Give him a stage where the audience praises and he will deliver good sound

He says some truth, that truth is deciphered in a booth

A prophet of sorts, a musical talent, a dragon who watches courts

A song that plays after all these Olympic sports

Which would stock a market that's about to crash

And puts ideas in our head that lead to cash

A gambler who knows he will win

A business that's something for kin

Because that power gained is a good thing

Where could you get this power from?

Could you get it from the higher ups? Or are you under their thumb?

"They" envision a plan that's only known to some

The only reason they know is because they have asked

These people that seem to improve really fast

Evolving and changing to something that lasts

A mass full of spirit and closeness that's hidden

Puts food on the table, a big chicken that's been ridden

A feast filled with pleasure of all your different senses

Which break down all sorts of different fences

A riot with pigs and rats and snakes inside

Distracts the place that conceals and hides

These things that are sacred I will never confide

Until my dream is planetwide

Power

Power is a wonderful thing to behold

Power is something that's worth more than gold

Power is something that doesn't go away when you get old

Power makes you feel charismatic and bold

Power is something that can never be sold

Power is something you can bend and can mold

Power isn't bad, it's the person that uses it

Power should not ever be handed to ignorance

Power should not ever be taken dishonestly

Power belongs to those that deserve it

Power is a tool, just like a gun, and exactly what beauty is

Power is something in which you can become studious

Power can be given for free or viciously taken away

Power is something at the end of the day

Mercy

Is this god, me, or the world around me speaking?

I live for mercy, this is what I am truly seeking

Forgiveness for forgiving one's horrible behaviors

We can all be somebody's savior

We can all get divine favor

Working together to overcome our disease

Would help me be filled up with this hope and this ease

I'd relax a little more with some rest and some leisure

This relief I find will always lead to pleasure

Sometimes taking a time out can be one's greatest treasure

The things that make me free decrease without some moderation

I wish I was released from all these unhelpful creations

I wish my future was full of sport, euphoria, and vacation

I think the cure to this is somewhere locked inside

Confined in solitary, meditation couldn't hide

The answers are here, are you looking hard enough to find them?

It will be fine if you just look a little more

Just wait and see, wait for the reality that's in store

Just think of what it does instead of what it stops

Relax and you'll see when the bubble pops

Repeat?

When it started, we took flight, but then we started sinking

Then it heated up, our people started roaring and drinking

Then we made mistakes, got depressed cause we weren't taking care of our self

We went to war and then we put our needs on the shelf

We started to fight for the oppressed and then we got integrated

We got really high and then we celebrated

Advances in technology blinded us with lies

We grew cold so we had to break our walls down to realize

We communicated better; it was becoming popular

Then we got bombarded by fear and terror

The fear was good because we learned what had caused it

Liberation is on the way, there's no way to pause it

Perspectives of a century you'd never think you'd see unless you saw it

The King's Praise

All can rise, if you want to glisten then listen

Concepts that help put any king in position

When you get closer to god, he can give you your vision

It's exactly like wish fulfillment or soul nutrition

A feeling that lights you up and then it makes you feel proud

He is grateful for a network that's hidden in shrouds

Nirvana is here, the music is loud

Ambitious at the moment, that moment is now

He strives to reach heights that are not yet achieved

The direction is up, that's all he believes

Focuses on a craft that he can call effortless

Forgiving the path of wanting love that is generous

Grateful for the work, it's groovy and it's right

Heightened imagination, it's nothing but insight

Lover of beauty, knowledge, truth, and thoughts the mind can hold

The king protects his home from the days of the old

The king runs his court, it's like an organization

Power is what he owns, a peaceful paradise is where he's stationed

He's relaxed and refreshing, a tranquil look will now be born

A calm and serene place, the court has transformed

Victorious, your vulnerabilities will not show

How can he be worthy of a family like this? I don't even know

He can affirm appreciation for his awakening glow

He realizes that sometimes you have to rely on divine faith

Energy abundance, this is what he really needs

Kind of like a song you feel but really it just reads

The ultimate winner, he moves worlds for his love

Maximum faith and trust for this angel from above

Benevolent and mellow, this is his game now

A shifted state of mind has gotten him wondering…wow

Connect

Give the drugs to the governor of judgement

Give the sex to the judge of the government

Give the money to the people of the environment

So we can have a place that's filled with beguilement

Exciting, entertaining, otherworldly is requirement

Being safe, honest, and helpful leads the advancement

Abandonment is not the way to raise adolescents

You got to be there so they can feel your entire essence

So they can learn to have their own views and a presence

That's a way to give the world a billion presents

A present everyday that is defined by your commitment

Protect and love together now that's what I call coefficient

And down the line the youth would lead us out of our delinquence

Before our ignorance can lead us out of our existence

I

Being seen is good, being heard is even better

The first word, something that is just one letter

A belief that will help make you become a go getter

The universe, the world, all these words in your brain

It all starts with I, which all of these things contain

Which is why pride is said to be the earth's biggest stain

I love me, myself, and I, of course I am proud

I see it now, should I say it out loud?

How could I hello other people be proud?

Mother earth and father time should always be cherished

Their love for you is something that should always be nourished

This is what helps you find your nature and your nurture

Something to think about when you think of your future

Church State

State and church are not separate

They split because they were powerful and didn't get it

They had different views but definitely play their roles and such

They did it well

One tries to control you and one tries to make sure you don't go to hell

I think it would be better if they switched roles

To try to make the other understand

That when they do come together, they will appreciate their other hand

I think that individually, these twin towers were pillars for our development

Externally you could say they are fraternal

Internally they're identical, and that will always be eternal

These two entities have created our entire world

The state just didn't know how to praise well

The church just didn't know how to raise hell

Combine these towers then they could make a solid government

An environment that has the power to create

A place that has the freedom to recreate

They would learn by building together instead of destroying the world around them

They would learn by having one goal that binds them

They would earn their things instead of taking from the other because they were really trying

I think it all starts from where they began

To determine whether the other can really lend a hand

They benefit by both talking to the one above, while giving a shout out to the one under

This clears up the catholic beatdowns and yelling thunder

Questions

This is my story, if I wanted to tell it, I would sell it

If I sold it, then how am I supposed to know how they will mold it?

What questions should I ask? What things should I do to help me complete my task?

What things will take me to that next level?

Why can't I understand? Why can't I know which choices are for the devil?

Why can't I look inside and see these beautiful answers?

Is it because I have to wait to be free from this life of cancers?

Should I wait until my life is filled with these metaphorical dancers?

Should I look inside, just to see how my mind advances?

I think that's a good idea, let me give it a few chances

Pronoia

Are most people good?

Is it right to doubt this persons intentions?

Do these doubts make my friends go on the offensive?

These delusions are so comprehensive

The detail I imagine make me so apprehensive

Something bad's gonna happen, it puts me on the defensive

Trust is something I want to willingly give

This fear in me is something I can never avoid

These words and references to things just make me paranoid

It makes me feel so useless and pathetic and annoyed
Thoughts break in and unlock my insecurities

External forces remind me of my brain's impurities

I'm brought down to earth and then this hell is where I freeze

A happy medium between this grandiose paranoia would be nice

Or maybe none at all would actually suffice

What did I learn from this? God, that was awful advice

What did I even do to deserve this roll of dice?

This obsession of perfection is my greatest vice

Is there someone out there that will respect all of my rights?

Grand Illusion

This confidence I am supposed to have rarely shows itself

Right now, all I ask for is a little bit of help

I want to be important and I want to be courageous

I do not think that this will ever sound outrageous

In fact this attitude I obtain will surely be contagious

I want to feel as though I am on another level so I can complete my task well

If there are some good things to be whispered in my ear, please do tell

I want my self-esteem and light to combine and break out of its shell

I wish I found a way to get this confidence more

Maybe doing something I never thought would help me be sure

Faith brings me closer to the source of our sorts

Believing and asking is important of course

I think that these words are a powerful force

They'll act as a tool and you'll know what to do

Your mind will have to have a beautiful breakthrough

Because this is the only thing that you will know to be true

What happens when you make faith and confidence combine?

I am sure you will be feeling something particularly divine

You can do what you need to do, you will be fine

That leap of faith you take will not put you in a bind

In fact, you'll see that this is something you always can find

Look at it all the time and you won't have to be reminded

Look at it all the time and then your eye won't be blinded

That blindness isn't necessary, it is not wanted or needed

That blindness will consume you and you don't want to feed it

Make this grand illusion something you can see clearly

Make this grand illusion something you always hold dearly

Character

This is a choice, a collection of characteristics

Desirable qualities, a fate that's in the statistics

A self-concept that you have to ascertain

White magic can help you obtain saintly gain

Adding up these qualities and installing them in your brain

Unlearn bad habits and create something new

In sync with what the world is offering you

Love of information, ask a question, get the answer with no limits

A chain of memories, take the steps to see emissary magus exhibits

Ambidextrous mind, energy that's contagious

Admire right and left cohesion and it will be outrageous

Formidable authority, an influence of love

Noble touches with a hand from up above

Charming reactions can work like a beacon

Ambition that couldn't even settle as a deacon

Can the master appear? A symbol of benevolence

This is when you advance in the highest of directions

Protect

There has to be something created from this blank space

It all depends on who you want to be your face

All these horrid events, they were never unexpected

It seems to me that all these happenings are connected

The places that were safe don't seem like they're protected

A place where kids learn, people run, critics watch, and friends dance

The next place is worship; belief was never about chance

Give attention to the places that provide these things; if you love it truly, the mind will enhance

If you don't, then you will know you're in the wrong hands

Worldview

I need authority so that I can help my family

This driver's seat is becoming more clear to me

I'll sit back a little longer so I can enjoy and get my thoughts together

These obstacle I face will get me though this stormy weather

I know that in the end I will eventually become better

It's always good to take your time up these hills

Imagine how much energy this instils

After that you can take on these mountains

I think that it was best when we worked together to climb over these walls

And when we helped each other up when one of us falls

What made me stronger is just jumping in that water that is cold

These dark tunnels I go through really do help make me bold

Heights conquered, I jump, and I will never turn back

I am at the top of this pyramid with all of the help I received

When you see the end, it was like we all had believed

This therapy was shocking, my identity is what I retrieved

I think this peace and happiness will somehow band together

They will march forever in this bloody stormy weather

After the means the calm will come without pretend

Creation is the only way those means become an end

Good Grief

Whether you're alone, or scared, or in a crowd

These are words that help, you can say them out loud

I can help my family, friends, and town if I am allowed

I can use my imagination to make a magic nation

I am sick of all the death disease and miscommunication

I can hypnotize with words

I can put others in a trance and that is all that will occur

I can have fun and sing and dance with people out in this world

I can because I've learned from loss and it has made me strong

I can learn from hurt and turn it into blessings

This is my story, I turn my confessions into lessons

I don't have to deny what has happened and don't have to keep myself isolated

I can have righteous anger that is calm and that is calculated

I don't have to make a deal with the devil to get out of the hole that I dug

I allow myself to feel sad, because sometimes all I need is a hug

This morning, I accept death, I won't sweep it under the rug

I understand that death leads to life and that that life's light will be bright

I can see that those around me will reach new heights

Symbol of Fate

These actors are trustworthy on this social path

You could see why if you would do the math

Make them happy and they will always oblige

Except with more fame they forget to look on inside

Do I even know who I am anymore?

Am I a combination of all those things that I wore?

Is it me or my character that these people adore?

Maybe I'm me with a little extra flare

Tick me off and I'll explode, only if you dare

I didn't think anyone would care with all this information that was shared

I forgot how to feel, my emotions are scared

I'd rather not ruin worlds that I helped create

I'd like to get rid of this button of hate

Because this button to me is a symbol of fate

Metaphor

There is always beauty when you think of a metaphor

Because when you think of it, it'll always mean something that's a little more

A group of words that mean something that can alter your states

Empowering your memory of similar fates

Reinforce meditation and be sure this is something that motivates

These insights that you see will be right between the eyes

Liberated, grace is freedom in disguise

Don't be doubtful, you can trust these suggestions

I'll hypnotize my mind to be sovereign and independent

Reflection shows that I can be grounded and confident

I don't have to pick sides but I will listen to the innocent

Superior secrets, listen to this

The things that you think of can give you limitless bliss

I urge you if you follow then you will be grounded

At ease, conditioned, and thankful to be founded

A new state, one with language that has true intentions

Study all the time and make these wonderful connections

Sex and music is like a fix it's like a drug

I vote the ass and elephant don't have to play and tug

Remember this when you come back home from far away

Think of when the only power is in what you write and what you say

The person I am, can I choose authentic people?

This pen reminds me of the truth that's inside a booth

I don't want to be sneaky or authoritative

I want to be knowledgeable and appreciative

I think all the glory should go to the dictionary

Because this lesson I learned is revolutionary

The singers and ballers can govern this static

Life is sport, role models always have fanatics

Comedians are loved because they make people laugh until they're nauseous

These medicine men can change up your conscious

Prayer

I pray to whatever gods may be that they are looking after me

I pray that source of knowledge does not make a fallacy

I pray the ones I love will know where they'll always be

I pray that my needs are met

I pray these human resources are something that aren't set

I pray that I will always pay my fair share of the debt

I pray the place I travel will leave me something more than blessed

I pray that learning will never leave and I'll get nothing less

I pray that I can pass these tests if I try my very best

Coach

Ball is life, it's a wicked excellent fantastic game

Con academy, my seeds are all growing up the same

Kind enough to listen to the team

Helpful example, play it right and the results will have to gleam

Open mind, I think the tradition is winning

Bodhisattva on the sidelines, crooked smile and always half grinning

Allegiant to the source and this is my declaration

Attack the paint and it will splash like exclamation

Excellent systems cohesive movements

Continual authorship interpolation improvements

Genuine accumulation and application of conjecture

Always refining and always referencing the lecture

Emphasis on teamwork, rebounding is in the roots

Help me improve too, logos practice, my feet have heavy boots

Overload your mind, remember this play

Pack the paint, color the canvas, and pray

Dribble, drive, kick, whatever you need for space

Sit on the rim, grab the ball, and find a pace

Come! Get into it, light up your mind

Game over, plug into the green, and love the value that you find

Teacher

Why should I do all this paperwork?

All of us can help one be secure, yeah, God can say that's a fact

Logic upside-down and trolls can aid one to react

Bookkeeper, for the people and all that could ail

Powerhouse trucks, I'll hit it right on the nail

CDs the south is warm and always expanding

The other side of it can be seen as just as demanding

The web site is seen and is looking to rise

Paycheck needs a boost, that's something I can theorize

Yellow chakra healed, am I good to take care?

Everyone is still different, the money and love is now there

Let me explain, other worlds are destined to help the peddle

Level up and heal so one can acquire the metal

Saving and going through, work together to paint a picture

Looking up, all of the hats that I wear is really just a mixture

Account for everyone, faces are easy to remember

Poetry in motion, winning awards in the December

Ask the question, only creative answers can come

Pushing self and growing is the motto for a sum

Take a breath and look at the ball go through the hoop

Problem solving always seems best in a group

Unified vocabulary, learning by the second

Bruh ... overcoming obstacles is in the next act I can reckon

A thread of aphorism, it's going all around

It's a wonder how seeds can sprout and then they can abound

Food

Divine partnerships, there is guidance all around

Meals of good nutrition is the mission that I found

Don't force it down my throat because that doesn't help with aid

Studying the source, it leads to grapes and lemonade

Eggs about to hatch and that's some really good news

For the sake of an example, search the engines for some views

Helps with the root chakra, it's swift and hears the dream

For now it's free for the taking, but later I want a dollop of cream

Delicious cheese consumed before one gets to rest in peace

Meat that's cooked exactly according to the recipe

Buns matching up, I wonder about the fee

This is what I have been praying for, please help me with the communications

Always referencing words with different meaning and connotations

Sugar, pie, honey, golden ooze that's running out

Sweet, salty, sour, bitter, my tongue is what will help me find my route

Red, chakra that keeps me grounded

Store all of the goodies just to keep myself confounded

Sentinels can see, make sure the answer isn't random

This is actually a gift for future use, a memorandum

Bend a little bit, cook up immaculate conception

Elbows in the pot describes the meal of inception

Extend the eyes to the final product of sorts

Follow through and see how other people contort

Incrementalism, the food is cooked for more than a sum

Concepts that help increase the gross income

What they want, giving thanks for all the bluffing

Even grateful for all the sauce and all the stuffing

DEVON GILLESPIE

Student

It's the miracle of mind, fullness is the word

Sutra-growing minds and has the range of a bird

The student surmounts the challenges, this is the only rite

Holism and word expansion gives immeasurable insight

Right now solutions are popping up like an accord

Exertion and expansion of the word is unmasked

Man raises self toward God with the questions that are asked

Look at the source document, it is easy to remember

Flexibility, highly qualified, multiskilled with aspirations

Processing and storage, collaborated representations

Promoting health and optimal well-being, its therapeutic intervention

Not to mention the dimensions sent and meant to spent a cent shin

Caring for patience, everybody is unique

What's the skillset? Does it rhyme with oblique?

Listen to me, I am looking straight at the knee

The grass is always green when you go to grass city

Because the internet is forever, the ports and land make elasticity

Mitochondria is the freight and the shipping is exact

Inland draft, I am an attorney in fact

Goo gull analytics, don't forget that all life matter

The devil can even help one climb up all the ladders

Book

What is a story that everyone knows?

A story of triumph, that's just how the world goes

I want to see too, let us jump to the conclusion

Home, body, work, relationships will feed the illusion

Positive aspects, look at my mastercard

Experience freedom, moments of choice will not be barred

Acknowledge everything, I can see all of the different sections

Look at the documents that make these memorable connections

It's like legislation or a point of exclamation

Celebrate others happiness so we can turn up all the stations

Characteristics of a relationship, or partnership, it's like complete devotion

Overcoming addictions and common afflictions, put the picture in motion

Personal mastery, the practice is complete

Enumeration starts with just imagining the seat

A clear message, with plenty of information

Resolution to the story just because we were patient

Successors constitute, the love isn't shrinking

The only thing I try to do is linking and thinking

That looks neat, I want to start making some sense

I'll end with a period, I'll use a comma in this sentence.

I'm the writer, I can conjure vivid descriptions

I'm the writer, I can lay out illuminated blueprints

Memorable, I just need to observe the conventions

I'll probably get a zero or some honorable mentions

Dogma, daughter, mother, spirit of wholeness

Have to fix the plumbing that is the goal in this

Problems to address, emancipate for future good

Dreamers start to create different states and different moods

We proclamate and litigate the word choice with some glee

Referencing hiatus, I see apostrophe'

Future goods, bill of sale, I am laying out some sails

Stark, it is hard to concentrate when one can smell the scent

And even sees the possibilities of descent

Write my will down, I think I signed the dotted line

Accession for the audience is something more than fine

Not a democrat, ideas are in the middle

Organization really manifests when one plays with the fiddle

Voice of an illusion, caveat emptor, look at my knee

The antonym of contraction will have to surely cost a fee

Sentence fluency, purposeful drafting and revising

Sharing, grading, canto, illustrious devising

Descriptive to the point, don't focus on the predicate

Interjection, adjective, this is what we are when we meditate

I am the preposition, I am the synonym

This narrative to me is like an angel and a hymn

Informational and technical, the business is persuasive

Sample of the index when the mindset is evasive

Self-reflection is important, it should be the one priority

Imagination of a sample, a transmission of seniority

I see the stocks and bonds are possible for commission

Look back, recall the piece, or aid the omission

A constructive notice, I should hang on to that warranty

Love for all the mothers is the only guarantee

Awake

Quotation, word of mouth, let's all ask this to make sure everyone is prepped

Transpose, how do you understand a concept?

Hyphenate, self-expression, deliver some mail

This is what happens when you drink out the grail

Individuality, the definition of a semicolon

I'm being used to show what follows, the definition of a sentence colon

Uppercase Delta, I'm just sticking to the superscript

Personal enlightenment, I think the world is kind of flipped

I have a practical purpose, Socratic method and identifying

Successful introduction, I just want to keep flying

Establish something new and start to see a line extension

Easy to say, spell, read, remember, releases all the tension

External influences, situational awareness

Turn the radar on, step one is problem recognition

How do you understand a concept? Should it be in the description?

I need a clear message, I need a clear question, I need a clear reaction

I need some valid words to understand the transaction

Food and water, purple reign for generations

Diversity and growth is in the communications

Continuous installation and idea generation

Simulation confirmation, phase to commercialization

Technical development, a drive to fit in the target market

A drive with benefits and clearly knows about the target

Make sure you eat the negative like a vulture

It's in a box and wrapped like it was birthed by our nature

Whole

All of these words that separate us

What are the words that liberate us?

It's time to look at the entire picture

Dimensions of light is what will help us not be insecure

We will beg for truth, the lie will be outta sight

Try to find actualization without a fight

Bow to the queen or you will be humbled

If we don't then the king's praise is something that will be crumbled

Appreciate the worldview, it's the answer to the question

The music is a drug, the sex and money will be destined

We're it, characters that can use good judgement

And can probably respect any form of government

Oscar mike, the scared receive pronoia

Again the truth is seen and the lie is paranoia

Sleep on it, find the results of the book

Go into that stream and make sure that you look

The family is social and they do it by choice

Use a little dark magic and a meaningful voice

Charge ahead, elaborate on the details

White magic is encoded and it seems to never fail

A reason to store and recover the environment

Connect to nothing and a church state will be invited in

Don't pull the trigger yet, but can this be something that you repeat?

The media will alter your senses on defeat

There is power in the grand illusion, it's a symbol of fate

Protect the metaphor and we find that prayer opens the gate

Have faith, this is now a bird's-eye view

Now this is something that we know to be true

Listen closely and we can hear the call

We can dream big and hope this place is free for all

Water

It doesn't come from a bottle, it comes from the fountain

Blue chakra that helps me see through the mountain

Strong state of flux, I can have capacity unlimited

Channel surfing, I am just opening up the stimulus lid

Flow and elasticity, a continuum that staves

Analyzing every single piece of the waves

Never interrupted, taking the easiest of routes

Pouring down and then all of the seeds will grow and sprout

Cold and hot, atoms focused on material

Study the divine and one will start to feel ethereal

Drink up all the knowledge and make sure one doesn't slip

The dripping and the tripping enforces one to get a grip

Observe and see the interbeing of fluidity

Investing in fidelity and crying for liquidity

Streaming all the truth and ache to owe someone a ring

I just want to see the water fall into a spring

It's pure and clean and wet until the sun is near

Evaporate for reign I think the picture is quite clear

It's gushing out, the cascade effect is like real lux

It's all around us and in a constant state of flux

Alter

Change the pair of dimes into something that makes cents

Shift of roles and jobs is hard enough to commence

An altar ignited, the treasure is right behind the door

I can choose the order of business because it's nothing I abhor

Observation is a solid way to learn

The attitude I want to have is something that I'll earn

The mental state I want to earn is under one condition

I want to have a lucid and supreme-like cognition

Open mindedness, a mindful mind of master monkey monks

Behavior can be changed to a habit of hard work

Personality manifesting into a defined young Turk

Do I have to prove a self-concept that's already known?

Do I have to see if it's something I can loan?

It's alright to feel alright again I am inebriated

The substance that is here has already been recreated

It's indestructible, it's pure, and it is here in a flash

Already done, all the vendor wants is cash

I'll receive an invoice and I'll thank the merchandiser

And oratory permanence will help me become wiser

Encoded

Word engraved in memory, the strongest ones will thrive

These things that are now seen took a while to compile

Utter importance, these are needed for the test

Focus, now opening the book is like a chest

The next time I read it I will be nothing less than blessed

I am grateful for the words, they make me obsessed

I am grateful for the words, its love of information

I am grateful for my past self, he helps the communication

Processes and prices, the value helps the population

Repetition is the language of observing imagination

Knowledge of results can help explain the top position

Chunking info into bits enforces easy transition

Hypnosis, learning secondhand from all the sources

Sleep, a psychic analysis of factors and forces

Meditation, a permanent change in behavior is the reward

Law, rule, and order is sitting at the head of the board

Planning for security, complete and error free

Perform and develop praise and the truth is what you see

Define the transaction, an accrued way of thinking is learned

Now I will see the desire to record the cash flow when it is earned

Preparation

Specific rules and guidelines that have been measurable for centuries

A process that is specifically used for adjusting entries

No more damages, I'll see a statement of income

Operant conditioning is the only way to learn for some

Beware of plot twists, reward is based on the response

An article that shows the book value more than just once

Looking at scenarios that are fed up on a plate

A plant asset is seen and is ready to accumulate

Expenses deferred and residuals will not be deterred

See the trial balance, accrued revenue will be inferred

Willpower and productivity, the consequence is forgetting

Repetition is a habit that is perfect for this setting

Noticeable progression, the hat isn't built in one day

The treats help you focus on organizational sway

Don't go off the rails, embrace the face for forgiveness

Strengthened with bigger challenges, an intercession is in the business

Genres that oversee the reign like a scepter

A region of words that can help one exercise the devout receptor

Government

Energy and flow is what I will be sending out

Once again what you do is take the easiest route

This is for the people and the ones sticking out

This is for the money and the business I shout

All we need to worry about is the going concern assumption

Informed decisions make it so your bureau can function

Only safe people surround me, they act like a precinct

And statutory law is something that will be linked

Assets abound, the council will be all around

Different types of kingdoms and different types of sound

Always make sure you fulfill the commission

An invisible hand can help with the mission

How wonderful it is to express a contract

This is a role you may have to enact

Don't forget sometimes it's all just an act

An implied status, right under a formal contract

I will apply recognizance to avoid the unjust enrichment

The market price is now clean and simple, it is written

No limits to growth, know that decision is unilateral

Listen closely because now that hearing is bilateral

No more brain drain, it's time to form a bond

Safe information, the diagnosis is blonde

I just need a letter of credit to get the banks acceptance

And maybe it could be a partnership of tenants

Choose to be heard with your communication

This can help one build a pretty solid foundation

The first thing you can do is use good form

Act like a cento, a line used in another poem

The actions are executory, it's the doctors' orders

A hospital that learns and has space for some quarters

Qualities of a good husband and father, I choose this path of mine

I choose this agreement, this marriage to the world is fine

Charge

Energize your direction, this will leave you empowered

Full speed ahead it's really time to move forward

Aphrodisiac, a lustrous gem with golden bands

Choose the solar plexus and keep looking at your hands

Act like a cento, a line used in another poem

Sometimes one has to hit the brakes, take a moment, keep going

Silver hair and whiskers are already showing

Adjutor or adjutorium aura is awesome of course

Transfiguration can always help one plug into the source

All I have to do is figure out how to mortgage

Things piling up, organizing for some more gauge

Regulator, motherboard, emblem, self-expression

Derive and mesmerize achievement and love innovation

I just want to know who can sing the perfect versicle

No lag in between, it always flows and it is merciful

Plug in, it's time to charge up the battery

Quality components and modification of a factory

Construct ways for makers to swim in information quantity

Strivers installation, all I want to see is property

Dark Magic

Invisible particles of pure intentions

Energy sharing can help with anybody's ascension

Four different types, it's an elemental view

Conceding to the light really helps you renew

I'll call upon the air to attend to my love

I consecrate that the earth will feel the sun's gold from above

And an altar of fire invokes the lady so bold

And that the water surrounding soothes the lord so cold

Chemistry between is not a null and void contract

Multiple open circles, I wonder how these thoughts will impact

Illuminate, awaken the forces inside

The darkness and the light is somewhere I can hide

I need communion, purification, protection, and grace

I need help, I need the strength to open that space

Going through the gate, it's like jumping in a well

A ship you can imagine will help some ring a bell

Victory is coming, the discipline will have to sell

Courage shows that magic can help you get out of a mess

Sometimes the spells can be your biggest success

It could help, it's an invocation of mojo

This space is what they call a numinous dojo

Identify the strength and even all the weakness

An opportunity to see the threat will be what releases

DEVON GILLESPIE

Lessons learned, everything is now coming together

Connect the dots and you will be able to see a new ledger

Receive

What does it feel like to receive?

It feels like when I smile giving something away

It feels like an idea that's popping into my brain

I will want to say exactly what is going on in that thing

It feels like general acceptance, it's the principle that counts

Faithful representation is what the value amounts

Needs that are met with laser efficiency

Long-term goals do not have deficiency

Transmit benediction through airwaves of space

Profit and knowledge of a subliminal race

A book that is written, the view is not narrow

The direction will only go as straight as an arrow

A basket of birds and bees ignite the flame

Achievement, personal mastery is where I will aim

Results

What do the results look like?

A worldview that can go with your sequential thinking

The family is secure, that ship is never sinking

The only thing that's cool is the love of the school

The media can help with organizational rule

A strategic plan, it's a secret to self

A book that you may just have to put on your shelf

Healthy food for the soul, the words make it satisfying

And tangible growth is something that is never dying

A mindset focused intently on the bigger picture

Even focused gently on the words of the scripture

Partnership of orientation, it's your duty of understanding

Discipleship that doesn't really seem all that demanding

Success and good cheer, it is easy to serve

Love the lesson now, the tests are graded on a curve

Answer

Right now I need to get into that creative space

So I can see another mirror pointing directly at my face

Sometimes it's hard to look at, but it has to be done

A world that's self-aware and then reflects to the sun

How does my present situation relate to the future?

Can this be it? Can this help tomorrow's story have some structure?

The only one I will listen to is the professor in a lecture

Can I relate to my team more? Can I still have time that's just for me?

Is it ok for me to pay attention to all of my needs?

I've forgotten what it feels like, to be aware of all my misdeeds

Is this a test or is this a chance to strengthen my resolve?

Is this a problem that my dreams can solve?

Elaborate

Explain, go over the details, take the easiest route

How to understand a concept is what this poem is about

Recreate the feeling in your heart, that's the first test

Thinking something new now is what I would suggest

A prompt that tells me to feel it in my chest

A topic that is in my waking interest

Pick one thing and determine if it's supreme

Find your hands, then you will realize the dream

Mentally settled, at this moment nothing else matters

I can be the one to open doors and climb ladders

Only love will come preceding the transactions

I just want to balance the equation with all of my actions

Some accounts are payable and they're in my jurisdiction

I am grateful but my fears are becoming an affliction

Determine what you can do to create sustainability

Look at the scorecards and you will see your value chain ability

You will not get enough, it's addictive consumption

Stimulus packages come with the entity assumption

All I want to do is figure out how equity can function

Motivation comes and the will makes more value junction

Sex

This is magical, I love how I can choose this perception

The only barrier between us is this plastic contraception

Give me more, I like the sensation

This is something I need, I enjoy this body conversation

Your language gets me thinking of the law of attraction

Do you feel the same? Because I can't wait to put that thing in action

Another metaphor, I like it when those things get on my nerve

Ending more with the emphasis on the curve

Pleasure senses, switching positions is my agenda

Massage the back and there will be excitement in the air

Which stimulates, seduces, and makes goosebumps out of hair

Erogenous zones, right around there it will throb

You might get excited because this thing is now your job

Seduction at its finest, I'm tempted to surrender

To a tried, true, and tested energy sender

Here's a tip, the coming from behind is now real

It starts to heal the mind and it will start to get ethereal

Get bad or be good and I will know how you feel

A plethora of needs, it feels good to be kissed

Arousal for this bliss is something hard to resist

I'm imagining something that is only my preference

Mut mystifying themes can really make a good reference

A simple release, at the same time I would encourage

DEVON GILLESPIE

I feel orgasmic ending when these two souls can merge

Money

The benefits I promote get higher in rates

This concept that is evolving will start to merge fates

Commitment to symbolism, invest in incentives

A gram of power, and then value dispenses

This is now a process of creation

Growth is a drug that heals an entire nation

Creative visualization can help the association

Exchange offerings and partners, lots of people talk about it

An image to convey, consumers tend to flock around it

Price it right and the results can be astounding

Promote the place that helps clean up the environment

Work towards the goal, terms of exchange is now requirement

Wash your hands afterwards, start to see all of the rewards

I just want to get the goods, degrees, rings, and awards

Start to link in, we can go to musical venues

I will give you my services in exchange for clear avenues

Form assets, keep going, and make sure you don't stop it

Time is of the essence so don't shoot down the profit

A message that can lead you to mind control or possession

Utilize the time, turn it into obsession

Focus on the goal, or the net, like a swish

Now anybody can ask the bank to loan a wish

I will account for anything I need even if I am a sprog

I'll even give a shout out to that poet in the fog

Don't be a liability, look at the bottom line

The next move is north, everything will be fine

Another team on the map, they're clawing for air

Retirement is great, insure that this place of space is there

Know what it feels like to jump start the process

This is a state of mind you know you can access

I am the soul proprietor, my standard of living is high I can confess

But learn to use excel and the worries will be put to rest

Revenue of rejuvenation, a blessing is always best

Music

If poems are feelings, then music is emotion

I need to see how music can put the picture in motion

It's a piece of the puzzle that will always heal

Experiencing something that you know to be real

Orchestrated creation, it's part of the deal

A weapon that can lend a hand

A weapon that can never be banned

A weapon that can take you to the promised land

No laws against feeling the rhythm in motion

No laws against experiencing the beat of the ocean

The music is everything, the love looks like ivory

The nothing is the note, like perfect pure ebony

The biggest stage you can think of can help you make some more money

Dancing with fire can be as sweet as honey

Solid as ice, the cold can be funny

A picture that's painted the numbers and terms

Written down, unless the memory squirms

No confabulation, I am conscious of crucial recollections

The music is here to help make the needed connections

Point Guard

See both sides of the court but stay calm in between

I can play the game and pass assists to my team

When I give you the ball, I am thinking of you

You are my teammate, I have complete faith and trust in you

Leader of the floor, control the tempo and the rhythm

A playmaker has to make good executive decisions

I can pay attention, I can notice patterns

I know the team's strengths and fundamentals is what I learn

Wings spreading, they are now equal in size

Power forward and know that strength is what you realize

Center yourself, you can ball and you can be the team's eyes

I only want to score if my team needs a rise

It's for the love of the game and the place in the skies

Last minute, there will now be laser focus

This is the time to not be greedy with assists

Killer mentality, it's time to get out of my way

Be careful with the rules or you can expect foul play

Redemption will come, only with the team

Think of how it seems when thought is more like a stream

Then you can take some of that on a whim

When you finish the only focus is on the rim

Drug

Music takes me back to when I was young

Sex takes me straight to the now and the fun

Sit on words, it's the easiest meditation

Love is when the highest high is safe with communication

Perception can be changed just give it some thought

Another world of ecstasy can be what is bought

A magic haze, I won't abuse the power

This is actually for all the empowerment I want to shower

An emotion that is completely in touch with the universe

Knowledge of joy will have to be something that is rehearsed

The best kind of drug is laced with giving

Smiles on a face will be my business of living

Memories of golden days will soon have to pop

My house, my setting is up at the top

I guess we will see when things start to shift

From now on I choose not to see a rift

The memories are saved and I think it's time to educate

Make sure you know what's safe and then you can elaborate

Socially acceptable, it's what they call a new state

It would stock a pile of memories full of fences

All that thing did was just heighten my senses

I can focus, I can learn, and I can stay present

I have a right to talk about my own development

Nothing but illusion, except I make that creation

No voice except my own, that's when I get the realization

A continuous prayer, this helps special images mold

A coincidence can lead you to a cave full of gold

Prepare yourself, remember your environment

Make sure it means something, and then get ready for retirement

If you are in trouble, go to that haven of safety

A strain that's euphoric, thoughts can be like therapy

A tool to use, I am glad that it's provided

Now it seems I'm not so narrow sighted

II

We've broken our spine; we have a right to be here

Work out and sleep and then you will never have to show fear

You have a right to feel it in your stomach

Eat good food with people you love so it doesn't have to run amok

You have a right to think because you are smart and you have power

Take some classes, read a book, and put the pieces together

You're almost there, you love yourself, you feel it in your chest

Smoke some weed, make amends with fam and friends is always best

Those relationships are loyal so you don't need a frog in your throat

Be a singing poet that would love to showboat

You start to see that you can trust yourself and others

Look at the stars and meditate with all your brothers

Now you know that in this kingdom you are the crown

That knowingness will never lead you to a frown

This "I" is focused on all your dreams and intentions

So you can see the quality of your meaningful invention

Here I am again, it's the middle of the night

Insomnia creeps in and the thoughts have no end in sight

Is that a good thing or bad thing? Should I start to pray?

I'm grateful for these moments that can ease up my sway

Is it just my body that is restless? Can I make that pain go away?

Can I focus on the dreams that are coming my way?

This will scientifically embody a new philosophy

The words are nearly perfect and they're right where they ought to be

These words will define your new reality, don't be scared

It's ok, calm down and know that these dimensions are layered

Fire and Ice

Two concepts, this is some left and right hand stuff

I am hoping that this poem will give you just enough

It's calm and collected, it's cool, and sometimes kind of stiff

The other is the opposite, it's wild and creative

If the fire gets too hot, then the ice will melt and create steam

If they both take their time, then they can melt together, like a team

If these elements were human, then they would have war

This war was with words, it was nothing like before

Eventually these words become like crack to me

Look at me just trying to find that perfect place of space and gravity

Maintain the special images that you have created

An endless conversation between these two is kind of fated

An element of this song is going fast and blowing steam

The other part is slow if they want to feel calm and serene
A song by the chosen ones, they've been chosen by us

They will make the perfect sound and give peace without fuss

You get what you give in this life, please trust

There is only one way for you to see this in depth

A look from above will help you see the perfect concept

Bird's-Eye View

Jumping in again, I can see the bottom of the pool floor clearly

It looks the same as up above, which is something I hold dearly

Summer is over, it's time to jump out and soar

True bliss is coming, and I expect nothing more

What if I fall? I see the worry kicking in

I'll take care of that later and put it in a bin

It's always a competition and I wonder who will win

But the end just makes me wonder who we're really with

Is it the woman, I bet if she confesses it then will be forgiven

And then a light will come because it's the truth that she has given

The man just has to get rid of his anxieties

Interpret this the right way and it could run a lot of cities

Belief is what you need to feel the greatness of societies

Relief is what you need to have the key to insight

Relax and you will start to see these things all night

The thoughts I am sending out, I hope they start making things right

I hope my friend is safe if he is in a big fight

I hope the ones I think of are always safe and sound

Because they are the ones who make my world go round

Dimensions

It's amazing when you think of what a day dream can do

It hypnotizes, it's a completely different awareness that's surrounding you

I want to fly, I want to expand my horizons

I want to know my borders so I can make some good findings

Although those heights are scary, I can see myself there

Anywhere is fair, I want to see something rare

The places I can see are most likely limitless

I would imagine that I can find peace of mind when I am thinking this

Think of when a line can mean multiple things

Take your time and you can see how much thought that it can bring

It's just like a character that embodies the same principle

How many different characters embody that same principle?

Your answers are important and the thoughts are what you need

Because thought is all you need for you to act on a seed

You're It

To you these words on paper could be just that

To me these words are more than that, they take up my whole world

It's hard to reflect when the day goes by in a moment

Of course love is on the mind again, somehow I try to lose it

I can't go through that right now, it really doesn't help my focus

It shakes things up, then there's no control of locus

What kind of poet can't even think of words to say?

Do I need to see more? Will that help me find my way?

Most will say that it's all locked up inside

I'll help break it out and it doesn't even have to hide

I don't even know where all these words can reside

I want these words to help me see the picture nice and wide

I want the words to ease out with a nice flow

This is something the world gave me, giving back is what I owe

Everything just has me wondering, will I reap what I sew?

I want to dive in that pool of consciousness and I really want to know

It's coming I can feel it, I wish there was some way to show

What's the first image in your head when all of this is said?

Will you even be reminded of something that you read?

Even if this is something that you can analyze

I am hoping that the truth is just not more lies

I am hoping to be connected to the love of this life

So I can have a tool to use to fight this common strife

I am calling it, this class of how much will be something special

All they have to do is be alert in their vessels

If we are truly connected, our minds will be on the same wavelength

Succeed or fail together, but we know that we are the champs

So many memories, looking back I wish I took that chance

We'll learn these lessons together, but we will be in different space

Or even different times, but this isn't tag or chase

Faith

It's time to have more faith in what will happen tomorrow

This day I swear will be the opposite of sorrow

I could be scared, but I am grateful for the now

These moments will be precious and all I will have to say is wow

That looks good, that smells right, that feels great, I will please all six of my senses

I am not sure how, but it will lead to nice coincidences

Looking forward to greatness, this is my only intention

I am hoping I can see the benefits of tomorrow's invention

I know what it can be because history repeats

At first I didn't like to look back, now I have some pretty good seats

Although yesterday was important, it's time to think of true feats

The answer is connected to the symbols and the signs

You will see when you have the power to channel your minds

Bow to the Queen

Bow down to her wholeness, a personality of perfection

True power that's just and complete with affection

Her richness of spirit is compelling and simple

She is alive, her people and pride will not wrinkle

A beautiful thing, the most powerful piece on the chess board

Her goodness towards her peers is what will always be adored

She is enchanting, she cuts and bleeds uniqueness

The truth is that she can be anybody's weakness

She is independent, and nobody will step on her reign

She uses meaningful words to help ease others pain

Bow down to the queen, submit to her will

Because her worship is the only void left to fill

Light

It's hard to find the words for the way that I am feeling

It's like love and holiness from God, the two things that I am healing

I want this more, I can't help but feel gratitude

The light that I am bathed in has really lifted my attitude

Thank you, I am really grateful for this divination

Work through me, imagine if that light could fill a nation

Imagine if that nation was a land of vacation

Imagine the growth and prosperity, it will get your heart racing

Experience transcendence, its self-love that you will be chasing

A mirror facing yesterday, was this in the plans?

Can this equation be counted on both of my hands?

I am speaking to all, can we figure out where we stand?

Can we really put our minds together and use our intuition?

Can my family and friends boogie down with the mission?

Let's go back to the beginning, let's see if its connected

Let's see if all the details have been inspected and dissected

It will only be respected if the truth can be elected

Your mind won't be infected and the love will be reflected

A land that's been promised or for a better word suggested

A symbol that's iconic, let's try not to kill the dream this time

In my next rhyme I am going to talk about the pyramids that we can climb

The top of it is where you will feel the gratitude and bliss

Today is not tomorrow, it's important to be mindful of this

With that in mind, stay aware of your own business

You never know what comes when looking to your own subconscious

A message that is learned, blend the sounds and you will be strong

You find out the teacher and the student were the same all along

The line was never there, it was imagined by the wrong

The only way to describe the universe is use one little song

The perfect sound, is it silence or a crowd?

The perfect sound, is it nature? Is it loud?

So many topics mixed together, I am having inefficient attention

This all makes sense in a different dimension